MAKING MANDALAS
FOR HARMONY AND HEALING

MAKING MANDALAS
FOR HARMONY AND HEALING

A practical guide to using spiritual circles • Laura J Watts

LORENZ BOOKS

This edition is published by Lorenz Books, an imprint of Anness Publishing Ltd, 108 Great Russell Street, London WC1B 3NA; info@anness.com

www.lorenzbooks.com;
www.annesspublishing.com

If you like the images in this book and would like to investigate using them for publishing, promotions or advertising, please visit our website www.practicalpictures.com for more information.

© Anness Publishing Ltd 2014

A CIP catalogue record for this book is available from the British Library.

Publisher: Joanna Lorenz
Project Editor: Charlotte Berman
Designer: Sarah Williams
Jacket Design: Nigel Partridge

PUBLISHER'S NOTE
Although the advice and information in this book are believed to be accurate and true at the time of going to press, neither the authors nor the publisher can accept any legal responsibility or liability for any errors or omissions that may have been made nor for any inaccuracies nor for any loss, harm or injury that comes about from following instructions or advice in this book.

CONTENTS

INTRODUCTION   6

UNIVERSE OF MANDALAS   8

ANCIENT PATTERNS   10

LABYRINTHS   11

CELTIC SYMBOLS   12

CHRISTIAN SYMBOLS   13

NATIVE AMERICAN MANDALAS   14

NAVAJO SAND PAINTINGS   16

HINDU YANTRAS   18

BUDDHIST MANDALAS   19

TIBETAN SAND PAINTINGS   20

MODERN MANDALAS   22

MANDALAS IN THE SKY   24

MANDALAS ON THE EARTH   25

THE HUMAN MANDALA   26

THE UNIVERSAL PATTERN   27

CREATING A MANDALA   28

BUDDHIST MANDALA: PREPARATION   30

DRAWING A BUDDHIST MANDALA   32

DRAWING A NATIVE AMERICAN MANDALA   36

PERSONAL MANDALA: PREPARATION   40

DRAWING A PERSONAL MANDALA   41

OTHER MANDALA CREATIONS   42

WAYS OF SEEING   46

COLOURS   48

SHAPES AND NUMBERS   50

TRADITIONAL MANDALA MEDITATION   52

PERSONAL MANDALA MEDITATION   53

HEALING WITH MANDALAS   54

CENTRE OF THE MANDALA   56

TEACHINGS OF THE MANDALA   58

AFTERWORD   60

MANDALA TEMPLATES   62

INDEX   64

INTRODUCTION

A MANDALA IS A SACRED space, often a circle, which reveals some inner truth about yourself or the world around you. In Sanskrit, "mandala" means both circle and centre, implying that it represents both the visible world outside of us (the circle) and the invisible one deep inside our minds and bodies (the centre). A mandala is a picture that tells a story, the story of a journey that we can follow from the hustle and bustle of the everyday world to our serene inner centre, leading us to a deeper understanding of the universe.

We all seek happiness and fulfilment, and Mandalas are a tool that can guide us straight to the heart of this search. In following the path through a mandala we are seeking to find the wholeness that lies at

◀ Some of the most beautiful mandalas can be found in nature.

the core of us, the stillness that always remains no matter what storms may surround us.

When we draw a mandala we can either create an image of our inner selves or we can carefully draw out an image of a perfect world and aspire to its expression of harmony. In creating a mandala we open ourselves out to all the possibilities that exist inside and outside of us. We listen to the dreams of our heart, mind and soul and give them shape and colour inside the circle.

A mandala can take any form. Any object when seen for its innate beauty can transport us from the mundane world to a world of happiness and fulfilment. By working with mandalas we may start to perceive the seemingly random reality around us differently and begin to turn what is everyday and commonplace into a journey to our deepest, innermost selves.

◀ Mandalas are a path to lead us back to our centre and our true selves.

▶ This 19th-century mandala is a Buddhist prayer mat showing peaceful and wrathful deities.

6

UNIVERSE OF MANDALAS

MANDALAS CAPTURE A MOMENT in time, embodying it as a circular picture or object. The circle is a potent and universal symbol of wholeness and eternity. The earth we walk on is a circular globe and the sun, moon and stars are all circles.

Throughout history every culture has attempted to under-stand its place in the universe. Each one has left us with a legacy of patterns and myths that describe the boundaries of its world and its understanding of the universe. Many of these patterns take the form of a mandala. Consider, for example, the Chinese yin-yang symbol. The Chinese see the harmony of the universe as a balance between the forces of yin and yang – the feminine and masculine principles of expansion and contraction, stillness and motion, intention and deed. This symbol perfectly describes the universe as the constant rising and falling of these two forces where neither completely holds sway. This is the way, or the "Tao", of being that the Chinese seek to live by. Its simplicity leads to a

▼ *The yin-yang is a symbol of the forces in the universe. Yin is the centrifugal, outwards force of the circle. Yang is the centripetal, or inwards, force.*

great depth of understanding culminating in the wisdom of the I Ching and Feng Shui divination systems. In following the path of the yin-yang mandala and living in harmony with the changing nature of the world we can be at peace with ourselves and walk in step with the rhythm of the universe.

The symbols and visual images inscribed in a mandala vary from culture to culture. Some traditions portray pictures of gods and goddesses, some use colour and shape, whilst others use natural objects. However, although each may use a different "language", the mandala patterns of all cultures describe the same cosmos as our own. Irrespective of their historical and cultural origins, if we let them resonate with us deeply enough, mandalas can lead us on the journey to finding our own inner truth.

▶ *A modern version of a traditional Hindu yantra.*

8

ANCIENT PATTERNS

Hundreds of thousands of years ago our ancestors saw the pattern of the universe all around them. They saw the seasons, the waxing and waning moon, the rising and setting of the sun and marked these events with mysterious standing stones and circles. These mandalas now form part of our geographical landscape.

In England the megalithic monument at Stonehenge heralds the passage of the summer solstice each year. This is the time when the earth is closest to the sun and gives rise to the longest day of the year. The complex alignment of stones forms an annual calendar. Our ancestors' way of life – from the sowing of seeds in spring, to the harvest at the end of summer – was dependent on those natural cycles.

Stone circles such as Stonehenge are a symbol of their world.

Human life, too, was subject to nature's cycles, and our ancestors built elaborate burial mounds to honour the eternal cycle of life, death and rebirth. These also form physical mandalas on the earth today. Newgrange, in Eire, is a good example. This burial-mound has a spiral stone roof and spiral-carved foundation stones. A single ceremonial chamber lies at the heart of the mound, where the dead were laid to rest. For most of the year this chamber lies in darkness until the summer solstice, when at dawn the sun's rays penetrate the passageway, illuminating the dark walls of its centre.

The ancient Egyptians also understood this wheel of life. The

mysterious pyramids were built as the final resting place on earth for the Pharaohs, who were regarded as living reincarnations of gods. There is a theory which suggests that all the pyramids form part of a pattern on the earth which mirrors the place in the sky where the Pharaoh's spirit would be reborn. At the centre of this vast mandala is a coffin in a chamber in the largest pyramid of Giza. This is the spiritual receptacle for the god's death and rebirth.

The symbolism from these burial places suggests that the centre of the mandala is a place of death and rebirth. It is where we all may be reborn if we are willing to let go of our old life. We must let the past die in order for the future to open up before us.

◀ *Circles of stone marked the cycle of the year for the neolithic people of Britain.*

▶ *The ancient Egyptian pyramids may be part of a vast design on the earth that mirrors the patterns of the stars.*

LABYRINTHS

The symbol of the maze occurs in every part of the world, as part of the quest for wisdom and self-knowledge. The twists and turns of a labyrinth are like a map, a path of life. In each moment we must choose which direction to take. One way will lead us closer to our dream, the centre. The other way will lead us further from that truth and will mean more footsteps on our journey. No matter how tortuous the path, however, we must never lose sight of where we want to be – at the heart and centre of our true selves.

In Greek mythology there is a story about Theseus and the Minotaur. This is centred on the legendary labyrinth at the palace of King Minos on Crete. The Minotaur is a beast, half-man, half-bull, which lives at the centre of the underground passage-ways of the labyrinth. Theseus, the hero of the story, has to find his way through the maze to confront and kill the Minotaur in order to claim his birthright and destiny as King.

An unknown people created the vast maze patterns of the Nasca Lines, Peru, thousands of years ago. The twisting shapes of animals and insects are on such a scale that they can only be seen from the air.

Many simple grass-cut mazes survive from medieval times. They form a single path, wide enough for a footstep, which weaves back and forth on itself. Monks and pilgrims would walk the maze on their knees in deep meditation, letting their steps take them onwards to the centre. These turf-cut mazes demonstrate the simplicity of life when we can accept its ever

◀ *The myth of the Minotaur reminds us that to find our centre we must pass the monsters within.*

▲ *Walking to the centre of a maze was thought to transport someone from this world to another.*

changing patterns and directions with pleasure and peace.

The Celtic stone-carved spiral mazes have many different paths to the centre. Although it is possible to take a short cut through the maze, in doing so we miss the subtleties of the triple-spiral path. It is only by changing our pattern of turns and not remaining fixed to any single rule that we can pass through it completely to the centre. This reminds us that a rich and interesting life is one where we are not fixated on our future, but can live in the here and now of every moment, enjoying life's twists and turns.

CELTIC SYMBOLS

The ancient Celts were a diverse people whose influence spread across Europe and possibly as far as Asia. They shared a spiritual heritage of beliefs from the Iron Age to the dawn of Christianity.

The Celts had close affinities with nature, the seasons, and the cycles of life, death and rebirth. Stones decorated with spiral designs and carved round figures, symbols of the earth, are found across North-west Europe.

The pre-Christian Celtic cross symbolizes the four seasons and the four directions – north, south, east and west – positioned over a circle of stone, which symbolizes the earth. With the advent of Christianity, the Celts took on elements of the new religion and their crosses became more elaborate. They carved fantastic monuments with elaborate spirals, animals and mythical creatures from the stories of the saints. These Celtic crosses were inscribed with whole sagas and biblical stories interwoven with older myths and legends. A favourite theme, for example, showed the passage of a saint from this life to the next where he or she would reach some kind of enlightenment.

These richly decorated carvings gave rise to lavishly illustrated bibles which were filled with the symbology of the creatures known to the Celts. Snakes, wolves, fish, peacocks and eagles filled the pages

▶ *Celtic knotwork is fantastically intricate.*

of these illuminated manuscripts along with delicately drawn knotwork. In the Book of Kells, each evangelist was symbolized by his own animal, and the decorated borders and letters of the gospels were a richly woven evocation of the wisdom written on each page. Every plate of the book was not simply a script but a symbolic journey illuminating a path towards understanding the deeper meaning of the words at the centre.

◀ *The illustrated manuscripts of the Celts are filled with meaning.*

▶ *The shapes and patterns on a Celtic cross symbolizes the four directions and the cycle of life.*

CHRISTIAN SYMBOLS

Churches are traditionally built facing east, in the shape of a cross. East is where the sun rises and symbolizes the resurrection of the spirit of Jesus and his gift of new life. The altar is always placed at the eastern end of a church.

Rose windows that adorn cathedrals and churches are examples of Christian mandalas. The intricate patterns of stone arches and flowers encompassing the vivid colours fill the church with light and beauty. Sometimes this light spills onto a circular maze on the floor, symbolizing the pilgrim's journey to the spiritual centre of Christianity, Jerusalem.

Hildegard of Bingen, who lived during the Middle Ages, had a gift

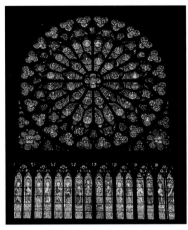

▲ *The window of Notre Dame is a vision of heavenly light.*

for prophecy and vision and communicated her visions through illustrations which showed the world, with man and woman as the pinnacle of God's creation at the centre. In one of her visions she saw God enthroned at the centre of

◀ *Hildegard of Bingen saw God as the embodiment of the centre of the universe.*

▶ *The circle of elements reminds us that to be healthy our bodies must be in harmony.*

a vast mandala, radiating a circle of gold with a great wheel at his heart, expanding out to encircle the universe.

Hildegard also believed that the harmony of the universe was a path to healing sickness. It was based on her vision of four principal human ailments and the four elements of earth, air, fire and water. She saw medicine as an image of the harmonious universe with the elements at the centre surrounded by the wind and the stars. Beyond this lay darkness and fire and the clear light of the sun.

At the centre of ourselves there is no sickness. There we are whole and healed, in harmony with God and the universe.

NATIVE AMERICAN MANDALAS

I WALK A PATH OF BEAUTY,
HOLD MY VISIONS,
HOLD MY DREAMING OUT BEFORE ME.

(Traditional Native American Song)

The Native American people traditionally see all life forms as an integral part of a single existence that surrounds us with its teachings. Every living creature, every rock or stone is part of the pattern of the universe. Everything contains a spirit, which is the essence of its connection with the world. To walk a path of beauty and truth is to walk in harmony with the spirits among us.

One of the most important symbols of the universe is the mandala of the Medicine Wheel. This cross within a circle represents the four seasons (spring, summer, autumn, winter), the four directions (north, south, east, west) and the four elements (fire, water, earth, air), all of which are contained within the circle of the

▼ *The Native Americans view the medicine wheel as a symbol of all the cycles of the universe; death and life, winter and summer.*

world. When drawn on a flat, horizontal surface it also represents the directions of below (Mother Earth) and above (Father Sky). The four seasons are symbolic of time, and the four compass points symbolize space. Depictions of particular animals, colours and many other symbols add to the rich and never-ending layers of meaning within the circle that describes the cycle of life.

▲ *Native Americans decorate their shields with symbolic objects from the world around them. They are not used as shields against humans, but as shields against negative energies.*

According to the Medicine Wheel, when we are born we begin our journey on earth in the East at dawn, a place of light, vision and new beginnings. As we learn we move to the South and a time of innocent self-expression and joy. As we grow further we develop our intuition and imagination and suffer the pain of growth in the West. Eventually intuition becomes wisdom and we journey onwards to the North. In wisdom we understand simple beauty and move into the East and so the cycle rolls on, until we pass into the sky as a spirit.

The teaching of the Medicine Wheel is that we will keep moving around the four directions until we can reside in the centre. Here we become one with the wheel of life and are in harmony with its ever changing patterns.

The Native American dream catcher is a mandala of the dream world. This is made from a single thread that is knotted into a spiral web and adorned with birds' feathers and decorative beads. It hangs above a person's head while he or she sleeps and "catches" all the good dreams, whose teaching

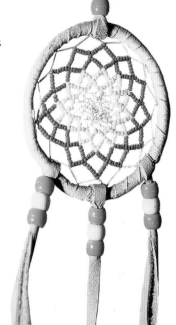

▲ *Sleep below a dream catcher to protect yourself from bad spirits.*

will remain on waking. The bad dreams, however, pass through the holes in the web and are released into the universe. At the centre of the catcher the person's spirit can pass into the dream world.

In a similar manner, Native American shields are created as protection from negative energies and also act as a call to the person's spirit helpers. The shield is an individually decorated circle made of skins, feathers, beads and threads. Each one is a weaving of the owner's own spiritual path and is a type of personalized mandala.

15

NAVAJO SAND PAINTINGS

The Navajo believe that illness arises through disharmony with the world. When we are not respecting our bodies or the earth, then we become sick. A medicine man (or woman) cures the sick by rebalancing their lives. The healer performs a ceremony, or Way, which is a carefully constructed pathway that brings the patient to a place of wholeness and releases him from his illness. The Way is centred on a mandala sand painting, the symbol of balance and harmony, and its story. The Navajo call the sand painting *iikááh* (the place where the spirits come and go) as they believe that the painting is a doorway through which the spirits will pass as they are called upon in the story.

The medicine man diagnoses the nature of the patient's imbalance and chooses one of hundreds of sand paintings and myths. The stories are deeply symbolic, speaking of the creation of the people and the earth, and of how we have been taught by the spirits to live in harmony with all life.

▲ *The Navajo see themselves as an integral part of the world, where every moment can provide some new understanding of life.*

The ceremony begins in daylight, and takes place in the *hogan*, a sacred lodge that has been blessed for the ceremony. The sand painting is created using string and other markers to accurately plot the shapes and symbols. The balance and positions of the spirit figures must be exact in order to create a place of harmony for the patient.

The base of the painting is built from sand, corn and pollen or crushed petals and, above this, charcoal and ground stone are carefully poured to give the outline of shadows and colours. The figures of the story are created as

▲ *The hogan is a place of ritual and ceremony. It is built and blessed with the greatest of respect and intent for healing.*

solid shapes with the image of
their whole bodies, back and front,
poured into place to symbolically
bring their complete presence into
the circle.

As night falls the patient
comes to the *hogan* and sits in the
centre of the mandala. The images
of the spirits are in direct contact
with the patient so that they may
enter his body. The medicine man
chants or sings the story of the
pathway back to harmony and the
patient listens and focuses on
understanding how he has
deviated from his path and how he
must stick to the correct path in
future to remain happy, healthy
and free.

When the story is told and
the patient has heard the lessons
and understands the changes he
must make in his life, the spirits
draw down the illness so that it
falls into the mandala. The sand is
now infected with the sickness and
it is ritually disposed of so that the
healed person is free to walk his
new path of health.

▶ *The sand painting is created
to exactly portray the earthly
spirits in harmony with the
human spirit.*

HINDU YANTRAS

Followers of the Tantric tradition of the Hindu faith use circular yantra in their meditations and ceremonies. Each yantra contains a precisely drawn geometrical symbol of a divinity. Every divine being has its own symbol of interlocking triangles, pointing up or down depending on whether the deity is male or female. The triangles represent the symbolic division of the universe into its primary forms of matter. Surrounding these triangles are circles of protection and a ring of petals signifying the attendants of the deity. This is all contained within a circular earth-city called *bhu-pura* enclosed by walls from which the guardians of the eight directions sit in ever-watchfulness.

Yantras can be either a circle, drawn and used flat on the earth, or a pyramid. A round receptacle is placed at the centre, within which the deity will manifest. Yantras can only be engraved on

▲ *Yantras are geometric symbols of tantric deities who are brought to life at their centre.*

eight so-called Tantric surfaces, gold, silver, copper, crystal, birch, bone, hide (including paper) and a special stone called Vishnu. Only these materials in combination with the correct colours will create the balance and harmony of energies so that the deity can

exist at the centre of the yantra. Yantras are considered alive with the spirit of the deity and must be born or "given breath" in a ceremony. Scents are smeared over the yantras, while a mantra, a simple phrase, is intoned over and over again. In the Shri Yantra, letters are drawn around the outside of the circle to symbolize the sound of the creation goddess, Shakti, to whom it is consecrated. In giving breath and life to the yantra it is believed to gain senses to perceive the world, and a subtle or spiritual body within which to live.

Yantras are sacred objects that can be used as the focus for meditation. The person seeks to understand and become one with the deity and so acquire self-knowledge and wisdom. In placing themselves at the centre of the yantra they become centred in their whole being.

BUDDHIST MANDALAS

Buddhist beliefs throughout Asia focus on the attainment of enlightenment so that we can exist in a place of perfect beauty in the universe in this lifetime or the next. The mind and body are taught how to walk in harmony, releasing the person from the constraints of ego and mundane desires. Traditional mandalas are a visual meditation tool that helps guide the true seeker to a path of greater understanding of themselves and the universe.

Mandalas are drawn to strict rules to create perfect balance and harmony. There are many paths to enlightenment and each has its own mandala and its own Buddha to act as guide.

Tibetan Buddhists use the healing and teaching properties of mandalas on a rolled cloth, called a *thang-ka*. These are usually rectangular paintings, drawn on muslin with a silk covering, and show the teachings of the Buddha, the wheel of life, the cosmic tree, saints and other spiritual guides in beautiful, richly coloured images. Tibetans also draw circular

▲ *A* thang-ka *is a painted rolled wall hanging.*

mandalas for meditation called *kyil-khor*. Each one contains a wealth of symbols and meaning. A monk meditates on the mandala by considering each symbol in turn, moving from the edge inwards. Their journey through a simple mandala might be like this: the seeker must first pass four barriers to enlightenment, which

▶ *Shambhala is the mandala-world of the enlightened mind.*

correspond to purifying fire, intellectual strength, the eight states of complete consciousness and the open, innocent heart. They then reach the four gates of the Buddha's palace. In each one of the four directions a protector spirit guards the doorway and must be faced before the seeker can finally enter the palace and reach the Buddha within.

The Tibetans see mandalas all about them. They see themselves as mandalas, they see their country as a mandala; and they see all beings, of any nationality, as potential buddhas.

TIBETAN SAND PAINTINGS

The pinnacle of Tibetan mandalas is a sand painting called *dul-tson-kyil-khor*, or mandala of coloured powders. The most complex of these is the Wheel of Time, the *Kalachakra*. This path to enlightenment and its mandala describe all the wisdom of the cycles of the universe and the healing that comes from living in harmony with its unceasing rhythms.

The Wheel of Time is a flat representation of a five-storey palace in which the *Kalachakra* Buddha lives, guarded by 722 pairs of divine male and female figures. Each pairing symbolizes one cyclic aspect of the world and the whole mandala is a single picture of all the cycles in the universe.

The sand painting is a crude approximation of the true mandala that can only exist fully in the mind's eye. Mandalas are a visual aid to help the monks create the

▶ *The Wheel of Time sand mandala represents all the earthly and celestial cycles present in the universe.*

complete world of the mandala in their inner mind and imagination. Once they can create the mandala in their head they can then journey through its mental barriers and pass its spiritual guardians in meditation. A monk will mentally walk through the palace and seek to pass each divine figure in turn as part of a meditation until he reaches the Buddha at the centre and an understanding of the universe moving around him.

The monks begin creating the sand painting with a ceremony to call on the goddess of creation and consecrate the site. They then draw the outline of the mandala in white ink following strict geometrical rules. The painting is created from the centre outwards, symbolizing the growth of life from a single egg into the universe that we inhabit today. One monk works at each one of the four directions, pouring sand meticulously from a metal rod, a *chak-pur*. For some sand paintings powdered flowers, herbs, grains and even ground jewels are used to change the spiritual qualities of the mandala.

This is the imagery used in the Wheel of Time mandala: the palace at the centre is built on the primal energies of the universe – earth, water, fire and wind. The ground floor of the palace contains the cycles of the earth, astronomy and human history. The next storey represents the Tibetan mind-body system of healing. On the third floor is the state of perfection for the physical body and mind, which leads to the fourth level of the perfect state of complete self. From this place the monk can enter the fifth level of understanding, as seen

▲ *The Kalachakra mandala is created from the centre of Buddha's palace, outwards, and is a symbol of birth and growing wisdom.*

by the *Kalachakra* Buddha, and become one with his state of being.

Creating the Wheel of Time also brings great healing to its surroundings. Once the mandala is finished, its role is complete and a final ceremony is performed to release its healing powers into the world. The sands are swept up from the outside to the centre of the circle and then placed in an urn. This is carried in a ceremonial procession to a nearby river where it is emptied, carrying the healing sands out into the ocean and around the world to bring peace and harmony to the whole planet.

◀ *The Tibetan monk taps out sand from his chak-pur.*

MODERN MANDALAS

In the last century, the Swiss psychologist C.G. Jung developed the use of mandalas as an aid to psychological understanding. He drew a mandala every day to express his innermost thoughts and feelings. Each time he noticed that the circle he had drawn contained a snapshot of his mental, emotional and spiritual state of being. It was as though the images were reflecting his inner

▲ *Carl Jung brought mandalas to the attention of the West.*

self. He also realized that the expression of the circle was universal, transcending time, place and culture – children spontaneously draw them, as do adults when they doodle, for example.

Jung came to see the mandala as a pathway to the self, and he began to use mandalas in his work as a psychiatrist to help his patients make deeper connections with themselves. The circle or sphere of the mandala represents the psyche that holds within it, at the centre, the true self. He dissected the meanings and position of the colours and shapes drawn by his patients. He believed that the top of the mandala indicated emotions that were held in the conscious mind, whilst the base of the mandala symbolized areas of feelings and thoughts that were deep in the unconscious.

The influence of Jung's ideas has been far-reaching and today many people are interested in creating mandalas and using them as tools for self-expression and discovery. With the spread of many old magical traditions through

▲ *This beautiful contemporary mandala is based on a traditional Shri Yantra.*

Western civilization, new mandalas have appeared. The Order of the Golden Dawn is a modern day group that combines Eastern traditions with Western magic. It has created a set of mandalas called Tattva Cards. They contain simple, coloured symbols such as moons and circles that are meditated on to develop the vision and experience of the inner self.

New paints and media have allowed modern artists to express mandalas in many more creative ways. Perhaps one of the most exciting and innovative forms that has been generated in recent times is through digital images.

Computers, with their internal patterns of algorithms and numbers, can help create some stunning digital images, sometimes incorporating real pictures. Three-dimensional computer graphics can bring the realization of a mandala into another dimension.

The information about the colours and shapes that make up a mandala on a computer screen is

▶ *Modern interpretations of traditional mandalas, such as this contemporary Tibetan-style mandala, are beautiful works of art as well as important tools for meditation.*

stored as a pattern of 1s and 0s. This pattern is in itself another representation of the mandala that can be copied and communicated to any other computer throughout the world. Beyond this, all the words we speak into our

telephones, all the emails or text messages that we send, all become pulses of electricity or light radiating around the world in a never-ending stream, a mandala of information. This is an invisible mandala, parts of which fly through the air to reach our television as pictures, and our radio as music. Other parts reach through the clouds to bounce off satellites in space, or pulse beneath the sea along vast cables of light.

◀ *This picture of dynamic light tracery shows all the colours of the rainbow and is a spectacular example of a computer generated special-effects mandala.*

MANDALAS IN THE SKY

Whether by day or night with its clouds or stars, the sky is a source of wonder and fascination for children and adults alike. Throughout the year, clouds weave and spin above us, forming strange and intriguing patterns. They collect, swell and darken with rain, and then part to reveal blue skies and sunshine. Their patterns reflect the motion of the earth, the oceans and the wind. We now understand that the flight of a butterfly on one side of the world can influence the weather on the other. Everything in the universe is connected and the clouds we see above us are a reflection of every drop of water, everywhere.

Winter is the season for snow and ice. As moisture drops from the clouds it freezes and captures in that instant all the motion of the wind and the earth to create a single, unique image – a snowflake. No two snowflakes are ever the same. When you see one on the end of your nose it is a picture of the world around you.

On a clear night we can see the movement of the stars as they turn around the Pole Star, Polaris. This star sits at the tail of the Little Bear constellation, unmoving in the Northern sky, and gives us our nightly compass. The constellations of the zodiac turn around this single point in the sky. It has taken hundreds of years for the

▲ *Each snowflake is a frozen, fractal pattern that captures the moment the flake was formed.*

light of some and a few years for the light of other stars to reach us. In every moment we are looking into a myriad of histories. The canopy of stars spread out above us is a vast mandala – an image of space and time, spinning around us, at the centre.

◄ *The stars circle above our heads as the Earth rotates around its axis.*

► *The sun is the source of life. We are composed of its energy handed down through the photosynthesis of plants.*

MANDALAS ON THE EARTH

We live our lives on a vast spinning planet. As the Earth spins, gravity connects us to the very core of the planet, keeping our feet firmly on the ground. We are each at the centre of our own mandala, looking out on to a landscape patterned with a myriad of symbols, shapes, colours and textures.

Rivers and oceans encircle us. Mountains, trees and tall buildings stretch above us, reaching to the skies. Urban or rural, our daily view is full of wonder that can enlighten our soul if we choose to notice.

A single stone is created over thousands of years by the pressures and motions of the earth. Water might pound its surface smooth, or

▲ *The seeds for a new life form at the centre of the sunflower.*

▲ *Tree roots spread downwards in a pattern that follows the flow of soil nutrients.*

grind it in the waves to form sand. Every stone carries within it an infinitely complex web of creation. Each one is a story of all the powerful forces that exist on earth.

A tree, with its branches reaching out to the sky and roots spreading down into the earth, is a living mandala. Through its size, shape and texture it is a picture of its growing history. It embraces all the moments of its past, both recent and long ago. It indicates when the sun has shone on its branches,

▶ *The spiral shell of a mollusc grows steadily outwards as it ages.*

turning them upwards, and times when rain has soaked into the soil, encouraging its roots downwards. The trunk of a tree shows the same story, formed as a pattern of rings, built up year after year around the centre – the moment of its birth.

As fruit grows, its bounty is dependent on what has gone before. The circle of the apple skin is the boundary between the present and the past development of the fruit. The juiciness of the flesh tells the story of the spring and summer rains and the seeds are the symbol of new life and a new tree.

▼ *When you cut an apple in half you reveal the mandala of its life.*

THE HUMAN MANDALA

Inside our bodies our blood, our organs, our muscles, the electricity passing through our nervous system – each tiny part of us – moves and works in harmony with the whole of every moment that we live, in unceasing rhythm.

The DNA strands at the centre of every single cell of our bodies is a map, a blueprint for us as we develop through life. We are the sum total of our parents and their parents and beyond. Our genes hold the history of every one of our ancestors and the instruction for the creation of our heart, body and mind, untainted by ego, fear or guilt. Within the

◀ *In the centre of every cell, our DNA directs the formation of every part of our body.*

centre of each cell we possess the potential to live life exactly as we were designed to do, in simple happiness and joy.

When we stand on the earth and reach out with our arms, our silhouette forms a five-pointed star. Around us is the air that we breathe and the land that we walk on. We use our senses to hear, smell, touch,

◀ *The human body is always at the centre of every experience that flows through our senses.*

taste or see the things which surround us. Our world is experienced through our senses, a world that we are at the heart of. In every moment when we are awake we can sense the beauty of the whole universe around us. We do not need to go anywhere special. It is always there, waiting for us to enjoy it.

In every step we take, we are surrounded by the mandala of the world.

▲ *Our pupils are circles through which the world enters.*

26

THE UNIVERSAL PATTERN

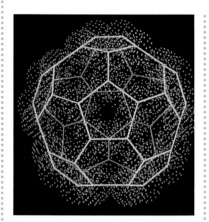

▲ *Everything around us is made up of a pattern of molecules and atoms.*

No matter what we are like — how young or old, how big or small, how rich or poor — we are always look-ing at the beauty and truth that is the cosmos we live in.

The food that we eat is full of complex molecules. When we digest these molecules they become part of us. The person we are today is built from the food we ate yesterday, last month, even last year. Each molecule is a beautiful arrangement of various elements of the earth, such as water, held together in a pattern that our bodies can read and understand.

When we look at the elements — such as hydrogen and oxygen that form the water that we drink — we find that they too are a mandala of little electrons spinning in beautiful, harmonious waves around a centre, a nucleus. Inside the nucleus, we see the mandala of the universe is also there. We find heavy protons dancing a slow stately dance, a pattern from which all the energy of the sun is derived, while inside them little quarks buzz around each other, and so it goes on.

Switching from this intricately detailed, tiny view of the universe we can zoom out into the vastness

▲ *Our planet Earth rotates around the centre of our galaxy, the Milky Way.*

▲ *Each ring on a tree trunk tells a story about every one of the years that the tree has been alive.*

of space. We see the earth rotating on its axis, ourselves on its surface, and the moon spinning around us. Then we look out at the solar system and all the planets turning about the sun in steady, eternal elipses. Beyond, we see our galaxy, rotating as a beautiful spiral mandala about a bright central core. And even beyond this we see the expanding universe unfold-ing and spreading out into infinity. The universe never ceases. Everything is dancing in a pattern around us.

CREATING A MANDALA

THERE ARE MOMENTS IN LIFE when we need to stop and look within. These are the times when we are feeling "out of touch" with ourselves, when our inner voice has become muffled or simply lost in the business of our everyday lives. In these times we

▲ *By using bright colours you can create a powerful, vibrant mandala.*

need to reconnect with what we truly feel and to find out what it is we really need to become happy and healthy again.

Creating a mandala can help us to find that still centre within. The art of creating a mandala involves turning our attention away from the outside world towards our true feelings, our hidden emotions and our inner universe. Every person is unique and each one of us has beautiful qualities. These may be evident or they may be hidden, but they are there all the same. By becoming quiet, by silencing all those loud voices in our heads, our endless worries, our endless desires, we can recognize the peace and harmony that exists all around and inside of us.

There are two paths that we can follow in creating a mandala. The first is the more

traditional way, which follows certain rules and procedures. This is how mandalas have been created for hundreds of years throughout the Buddhist world. If we sit and follow the elaborate steps we will create a picture of perfect balance. By following the intricate rules of mandala making, we can come a little closer to our inner selves. We can keep these mandalas for when we need to focus on our inner world, or destroy them when they have taken us to where we needed to be.

The second method is more spontaneous, free-flowing and less structured than the traditional approach. In this type the mandala is not planned. It is more a question of picking up a pen and simply drawing. This method is very useful for giving us a window into our inner selves. Through what we create, we can begin to see where we need to heal. Sometimes the very act of drawing a mandala is enough to bring us to a place of peace and harmony with the world.

▶ *We can become more harmonious within ourselves by reflecting the balance of the mandala's circle.*

BUDDHIST MANDALA: PREPARATION

When we create a traditional mandala, we are working towards making a picture of perfect peace, harmony and balance. It is therefore important to start by creating the right space inside and outside of us.

The drawing of a mandala begins with preparation of the mind and body. In Tibet, monks will begin by meditating and fasting for three days before embarking on a mandala painting! Although we won't go to such measures, we can at least follow some simple steps. These are to open ourselves to the stillness and balance that we want to come into our lives. Each step is as important as those taken with pencil and paper.

Begin by selecting a suitable place to draw the mandala. It must be somewhere that you will not be disturbed and where you feel at peace.

Focus on the feelings of harmony and balance you want to bring into the space. You may want to ask the spirit of your particular faith to help you. Fill your space with

beautiful music or burn incense and candles to help create a sense of peace.

When following these steps try and take deep breaths, right from the bottom of your belly, imagining your whole body filling up with light. As you breathe out imagine that the air you are releasing contains all your worries and anxieties. Let your mind become quiet and still.

Imagine that the music or incense is reaching into all the corners of the room and dissolving any dark areas into light. Picture your space bright and clear around you.

Look down at your hands, they are your finely tuned instruments for bringing the mandala into being. Shake them to loosen the wrists. Then clench them into a ball and release to

◀ *Before you make a mandala make sure that you are wearing comfortable clothes and that your immediate surroundings are peaceful and relaxing.*

stretch the palms and fingers fully. Clench and stretch a few times, feeling the blood and life flow through your hands. Gently massage each finger right to the tip. You will feel your hands almost grow as they become energized.

Sit in the place you have chosen and close your eyes. Keep your back straight and your body relaxed. Now you are ready to open your eyes. Consider the size of mandala you want to create and draw the outer circle using a pencil and compass.

Look at that circle. Now close your eyes and see it in your mind's eye. Look at the emptiness at its centre and imagine how it will be filled. Think about the journey you are describing, the journey from the outside of the mundane world to the peace at the centre of the circle. Imagine leaving the hustle and bustle of the everyday world and visualize rivers of stress and anxiety leaving your body. Think about the peace and tranquility that awaits you. Feel how close you are to the centre already.

Open your eyes, pick up your pencil and begin.

BREATHING EXERCISE
Follow this excercise to relax and unwind

1 Stand with your feet hip-width apart and your arms hanging loosely.

2 Breathe in slowly through your nose as you slowly raise your arms outwards and upwards.

3 Continue raising your arms as you breathe in until your hands meet above your head.

4 Breathe out from your mouth and slowly lower your arms as you return to the start position.

DRAWING A BUDDHIST MANDALA

You will need:
COMPASS
PENCIL
RULER
LARGE SHEET OF PAPER
COLOURED PENS OR PAINTS

The following steps lead to a simplified Tibetan Buddhist mandala. The geometric rules follow similar patterns to those normally used and some traditional symbols are used, although you could personalize your mandala by using your own symbols. The use of the ruler is limited to finding the mid-points, so the mandala can be drawn to any scale.

COLOURS AND SYMBOLS
Once the guide markings are complete you can begin considering the colours and symbols you wish to use to fill the mandala.

The five traditional colours are white, yellow, red, green and dark blue. Sometimes gold is also added for decoration and each colour has many layers of meaning.

Within the Inner Palace sits the central Buddha, who is both the representation of an enlightened being and ourselves when we are happy, healthy and free. The lotus flower with its eight petals is used by Buddhists to signify this state. The lotus grows in mud yet produces a beautiful flower.

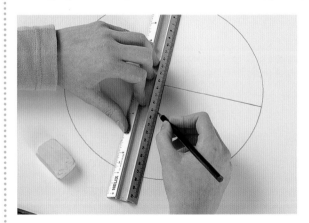

1 Draw two perpendicular lines to form a cross through the centre of the circle that you pre-prepared.

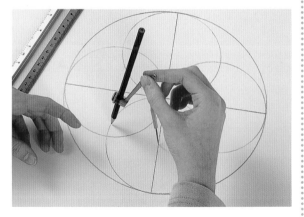

2 Mark the mid-point of each of the four arms of the cross and then draw four circles from each of those points, with a diameter the same length as each arm.

The four directions within the palace signify the cycles of the earth and time. They remind us that the wheel of life is always turning and each step on the wheel can take us closer to the centre if we choose.

The foundations of the palace are the primal elements which make up the universe and from which we are all ultimately made. From the palace down there is the yellow of earth, the white of water, the red of fire and the blue of wind.

Protective spirits, or doorkeepers, bar entry to the palace in each direction. Only those who approach with pure intent may pass. A traditional symbol that marks this space is the eight-spoked Dharma Wheel. Each one of the spokes represents part of the path to enlightenment: right belief, right resolution, right speech, right action, right living, right effort, right thinking and right peace.

Finally there are four outer barrier circles, indicating key stages through which we must pass. The outermost of these is a ring of fire, symbolizing the flames of purification which burn away ignorance. Moving in is a ring of diamonds, indicating light and illumination of the mind as well as the mental strength and endurance needed to reach the centre. Next there is a circle divided into eight burial grounds. These indicate the eight states of consciousness through which we must pass: seeing, hearing, tasting, smelling, body awareness, thinking, self-awareness and basic consciousness. The fourth barrier is a circle of lotus leaves. These symbolize the process of emotional rebirth that we have embarked upon.

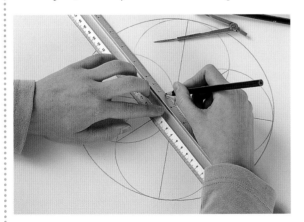

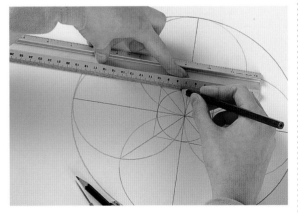

3 Draw the two perpendicular diagonal lines that connect the intersections of the circles and the centre. The two crosses together form the eight directions.

4 Mark the mid-point of each of the four directions of the second cross and draw a square to connect them together. This forms the walls of the central palace. Now draw the circle inside that square. ▶

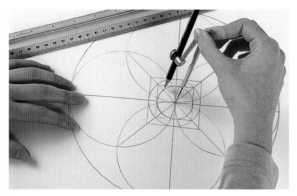

5 Draw the square that fills the inner circle and then a circle that fills that square. This final circle is the seat of the Buddha at the centre of the mandala.

6 Along each direction of the first cross, mark the mid-point between the palace and the circle edge. Mark the mid-point between this on either side, repeating the subdivision four times. Join the four marks beyond the palace to form four outer squares. These are the primal foundations of the palace.

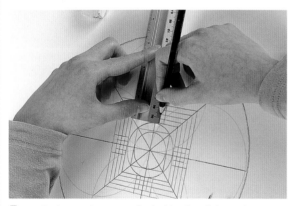

7 Mark the mid-point of a half-side of the palace square for each of the eight half-sides. Subdivide again and draw the four gates to the palace by connecting the outer marks with the outer foundation of the palace and the inner marks with the next foundation.

8 Draw four semi-circles with their centres at the middle of the outer foundation line and their width the distance to the gates. The outer semicircle, drawn to the distance of the palace, is the area of the spirit that protects entry to the palace.

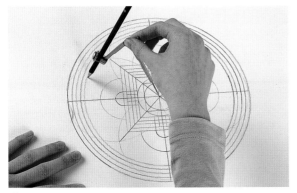

9 Join the four marks within the circle edge to form four inner circles. These are the four barriers to enlightenment.

10 Now you can begin to paint your mandala. Start painting at the centre, finishing with the fourth barrier. You can either use the colours of a traditional Buddhist mandala – white, yellow, red, green and dark blue – or colours which you feel best express the symbolism of your mandala.

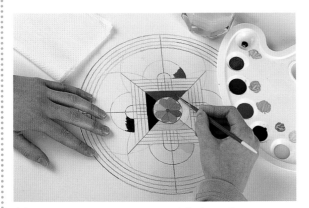

11 Continue painting the mandala from the centre to the outside rings. As you paint, remember the symbolism of each of the geometric shapes.

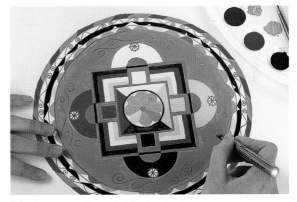

12 Once you have finished painting your mandala you can either lay it on the floor and use it as a tool for meditation, frame it and hang it on the wall, or give it away as a gift to a friend or loved one.

DRAWING A NATIVE AMERICAN MANDALA

You will need:
COMPASS
PENCIL
RULER
LARGE SHEET OF PAPER
COLOURED PENS OR PAINTS
NATURAL MATERIALS – RICE,
LEAVES, STONES, GRASSES ETC.

The Navajo created sand paintings as part of a healing ceremony. This painting is based on a sequence used in a creation myth and ceremony called the Blessingway. It celebrates the coming into the world of abundance and life represented by the four sacred crops – tobacco, corn, squash, and bean. It is performed to celebrate or bring about a turning point in someone's life.

The shapes in the sand painting are all highly symbolic. The centre circle represents the cosmic lake from which all life emerged and from where we can be purified and reborn, while the

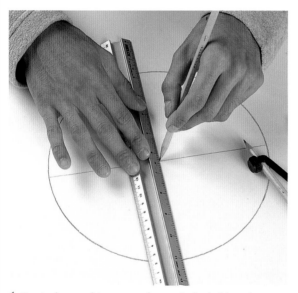

1 Begin by marking out a large circle (with at least a 15cm radius). This is the rainbow goddess who surrounds the universe. Draw in two perpendicular lines through the centre so that you form a cross. This is the basic Medicine Wheel.

2 Mark the mid-point between two directions and repeat this around the circle. You can now draw in the other four directions.

outer circle is the boundary of the earth, where it meets the sky. Boundaries between earth and water, and shapes representing clouds and mountains are also included. The fan shapes to the north and south represent tobacco and squash plants respectively, the zig zag line to the west represents the bean plant, and the plant to the east is the sacred corn plant. Each plant has leaves and fruit –

tobacco and squash have their fruit on the circumference of the outer circle. The beans hang down from the leaves in the west, and corn grows upwards in the east. The Navajo believe that only positive spirits may enter through the east.

Traditionally the Navajo use only living materials such as cornmeal, crushed flowers and pollen to create the Blessingway, so you may want to use grains

such as rice or oats, or leaves, or stones, although you may find it easier to work with paint, or coloured pens. The Navajo use different colours for each of the four directions. These represent the different stages of the day – dawn, midday, twilight and night. As you paint the Blessingway mandala remember it is a celebration of your unique life.

3 Draw a small circle at the centre of the mandala surrounded by an outer one. This represents the cosmic lake from which all life comes. Follow your instincts as to the diameter of this inner circle. Now draw an outer circle close to the boundary circle.

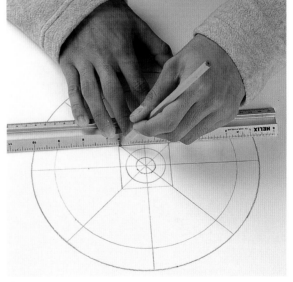

4 Next draw a square a small distance away and separated from the central circle. This marks the boundary of where the earth meets the life-giving waters of the cosmic lakes.

▶

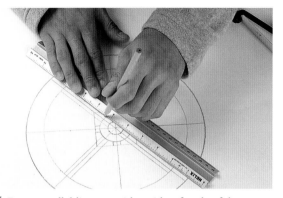

5 Draw parallel lines on either side of each of the four secondary directions. Using that same distance, draw small lines to connect the inside of the square to the circle on either side of each of the four primary directions.

6 Connect the intersection of the parallel lines with the square to create a triangle. Using the same dimensions, draw three more triangles along each direction towards the outer edge of the mandala. These are the clouds of the sky, which bring rain.

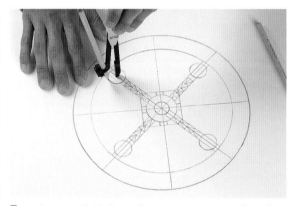

7 At the top of this line of triangles draw a small circle with its centre on the direction line and cross it to create a miniature Medicine Wheel. Repeat this for all four secondary directions. These are the four mountains of the Navajo world.

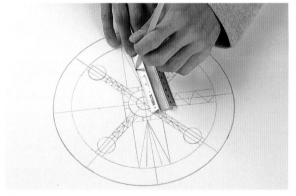

8 Draw a guideline the width of the second circle and repeat on the other side. In the north, begin from the centre point of the square and draw a line to the intersection of the guideline with the outer circle. Do the same midway between this and the direction line and repeat on the other side to make a fan shape.

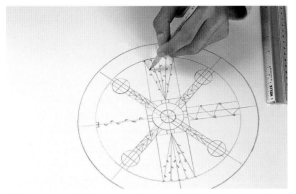

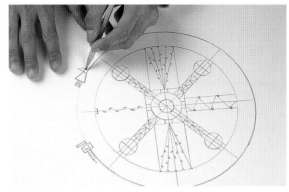

9 Draw in guidelines running parallel to the inner circle in the west direction. Starting from the centre of the square on that side, draw a zigzag line to the top. Begin adding leaves to the plant in the east.

10 Finally, open the mandala in the east. You may want to invite some spirits or good thoughts to come into the centre of the mandala as you do so. Draw a stylized head and body to represent the rainbow goddess at each end of the opening.

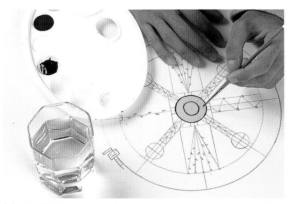

11 To fill the sand painting you can use any materials or painting media you choose.

▶ *The Blessingway sand painting celebrates the world and all its abundance: the flow of life, death and rebirth which we are part of.*

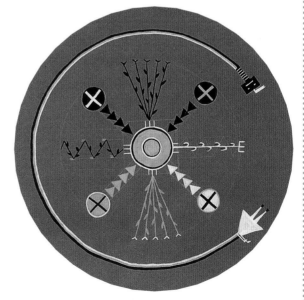

PERSONAL MANDALA: PREPARATION

The drawing of a personal mandala is a spontaneous act of expression from our inner self. However, it is important to spend a few moments focusing on the part of ourselves which we want to get in touch with and bring to the surface.

First gather the materials you will need. Having a pad of paper handy and a pack of pastels or crayons will save time when the moment to draw comes upon you. Other materials that are expressive are watercolours, oil paints and charcoal as these can allow soft and fluid marks to be drawn, reflecting a wider range of emotions than, say, the hard line of a pen. Coloured paper can add an extra element of expression.

Next find a quiet place to be alone in peace for a while.

▲ *Use different medium for different mandalas. Only through experimenting can you find the best medium for your personality.*

Sit down in front of your paper and materials and use a compass or a plate to draw the outline of a circle in the centre of your paper. Close your eyes for a moment. Sit with your back straight and breathe in slowly through your nose and out again. Try not to think of anything in particular.

When thoughts come to you, don't follow them but just let them fade away. Take ten slow breaths and let your mind come to rest.

Now in your mind's eye imagine the circle you have drawn. Imagine what shapes you could fill it with and the colours you would choose. Open your eyes and pick up your brush or pencil and begin.

◀ *Be expressive and experimental with whatever media you use to paint your mandala.*

▲ *Find or create a place of peace away from the hustle and bustle of everyday worries.*

DRAWING A PERSONAL MANDALA

Don't plan your mandala. Allow yourself to put the pencil wherever you feel is the right spot on the paper. Pick up paints or pencils on a whim and draw whatever comes to mind in that moment. Remember that you can change the speed and pressure with which you move your hand. You can do anything, even tear holes in the paper!

As patterns begin to emerge you may find that you add layers of colours. Feel free to use your hands and parts of your body to smudge, imprint and outline shapes in the circle. Other parts of you may want to speak as much as your hands! Fill the circle completely. Remember that whatever you do it is right, there is no wrong personal mandala.

MEDICINE WHEEL PICTURE
Another way to get at your deeper emotions is to create a Medicine Wheel or Celtic Cross picture. Take a large piece of paper and draw a circle. Focus on the circle and use thick water-based paints to spread

colour across the mandala. Now fold the paper in half through the centre and press down firmly on it. Push the paint down and around. Pull the sides apart and then fold it again through the centre but perpendicular to the last fold. Press down on the mandala wherever you feel the

▲ *Let yourself be free to spread colour and shapes all over your mandala; suspend any sense of asthetics and just express!*

need. Finally, open up the paper to reveal the circle of the mandala and the cross patterns and colours within it.

OTHER MANDALA CREATIONS

There are an enormous variety of ways to create interesting mandalas that you can put in a special place to remind you of your connection with the world and its beauty. Here are some ideas:

LIVING MANDALAS

Using materials that give us life can be very significant. Dried simple foods, such as rice grains, oats, seeds, lentils, beans, pasta and flour can all be added to a circle to create complex textured shapes. Find somewhere flat and smooth to work. Use chalk or a soft pencil to mark out the circle and any patterns or guidelines you want to express. Working from the centre of the circle outwards, pour in or place the food materials. Think about the depth of the patterns and the textures and shapes of the ingredients. For example pasta shapes could be made into a spiral pattern, or oats could be piled into symbolic clouds and mountains.

▶ *A spiral of life in grains and beans. Food is our source of energy and creation.*

◀ *What we eat renews us daily. Food comes in many shapes, textures and colours; it is an immediate and integral part of our connection to the world, a living palette for us to create a personal mandala.*

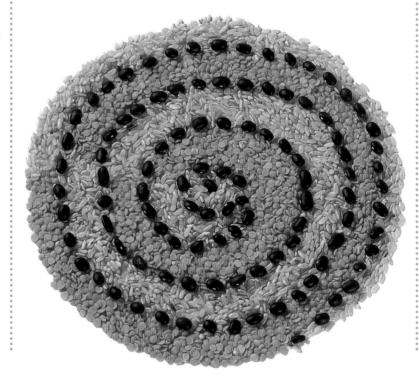

CREATING A ROSE WINDOW MANDALA
To bring a little illumination into your life you can create a translucent rose window.

1 Cut out identical-sized circles from coloured tissue papers and from a single sheet of paper. Put one tissue paper circle aside. Fold the other tissue circles in half and in half again. Do this twice more until you have a thin folded segment. Now cut out bold and simple patterns along all the edges, especially at the centre.

2 Fold and cut the paper circle in the same way as you did with the tissue paper circles. Make this the most simple pattern, with the most open spaces. Unfold the paper and tissue circles. Each will have a unique pattern and be a different mandala.

3 Put the paper circle on the top to act as a mask and then layer the tissue circles below it. Place the final uncut tissue circle at the bottom. Bind the layers together with a very small amount of glue, or sew them with coloured thread at points around the circle.

▶ *Hang the rose window mandala in front of a window or strong light source. Its rich pattern of shapes and colours can brighten any room. Looking through the rose window can remind us of the intricate beauty of the world, and that within ourselves.*

CREATING A SAND MANDALA
Use the templates on page 62-63 as guides.

1 Draw an outline of the pattern you want to fill with sand. Initially use simple, bold shapes.

2 Pour the sand, slowly and carefully, into the pattern. Use your finger to push it into the exact shape.

3 Sand is delicate and easily disturbed. You will need to remain focused and relaxed to the end.

4 Once the sand mandala is complete you can release its beauty into the world by blowing it away.

▲ *Take inspiration from the colours, patterns and textures in the world around you.*

▲ *The infinite variety of colours and shapes means that every leaf mandala will be unique.*

▲ *You can even make mandalas from store cupboard materials, such as dried spices.*

EARTH MANDALAS

These are particularly effective for outdoor display. Gather a selection of dried flowers, leaves, twigs, stones and other outdoor material. Begin by using the twigs to make an outline of the Medicine Wheel, the cross within the circle. Then use flowers and leaves to make

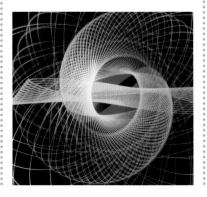

symbols in each one of the segments. An effective motif might be to have each one representing a different season. Stone mandalas, embedded in sand, can look stunning. A simple yin-yang symbol, done in light and dark pebbles, is an effective and lasting reminder of balance and harmony throughout the globe, as well as being a stylish addition to your garden.

◀ *A mathematically defined mandala, created inside a computer, follows the same rules as the world around us.*

▶ *Starfish are a striking example of naturally occuring mandalas.*

MANDALAS IN THE HOME

Finally, some other ideas for mandalas include cake decoration, collage, clay modelling, papier mâché, computer graphics, photography and embroidery. Find a mandala that expresses your deepest feelings and let its colours and shapes fill your senses.

WAYS OF SEEING

L OOKING DEEPLY INTO the circle of a mandala
means that we must look deeply into ourselves.
It can sometimes takes courage to study the picture
in front of us and see the storms and turmoil as well
as the peace and beauty that exists at our centre.

By studying a mandala in sufficient detail,
we can connect with our inner selves and look
out from the centre of our being. A mandala may
be elegant and intricate, laden with symbols and
vibrating with colour, or it may be simple and
sparse. Either way it contains its own wisdom and
truth. To unlock its secrets we must look beyond
the first superficial impression and appreciate the
detail within each tiny aspect of the pattern. If
we understand the message of each symbol, shape
and colour it will help change something inside
of us and bring us closer to a place of peace.

This intricate way of seeing, of always
looking more deeply into things, brings an
original and fresh way of experiencing the world
around us. Look more closely at a tree and you
will see the patterns of moss over its bark. Study
the moss and there you will notice water droplets
trapped in its rough surface. There is always more
to see, and this is the way with mandalas.

▲ *Plants surround us in gardens and in the house, but
looking closer we see how each leaf and petal has its own
pattern of intricate veins.*

The more we look the more we can
see and comprehend, and we can use this
understanding to take action and make changes
in our lives. When we see what makes us happy
we can alter our course in life to follow that
happiness. Mandalas can tell us, without sympathy
or restraint, the truth of where we stand at any
moment and we can allow that honesty to
permeate our lives.

▶ *The spiral pattern of a galaxy is the same pattern as the
strands of a spider's web.*

COLOURS

RAINBOW

The rainbow is an especially beautiful colour symbol. Red, orange, yellow, green, blue, indigo and violet arranged in sequence, together make up the colour spectrum. It literally contains all the colours under the sun, without which there would be no life. It is created by the elements of fire and water – the rainwater in the air refracts the fire of the sun. It is a symbol of wholeness and hope, arching through the sky, leading us to the fabled pot of gold.

COLOUR WHEEL

The colour wheel is made up of the primary colours – red, yellow and blue – and the secondary colours – orange, green and purple. Certain colours work together to bring balance and harmony to our lives. Each colour has its own meaning and represents different areas of our lives.

RED This is the colour of blood and of life. It is the colour of pain and passion, which comes with the initiation of change.

YELLOW Precise and optimistic, clear and incisive decisions. The whirling, intellectual, rational side of our being.

BLUE A place of stillness and strength, tranquility and calm from which we express our dreams and our purpose.

ORANGE This represents right beginnings and the determination to move forward into the light and away from the dark.

▲ *All the colours of the rainbow are reflected in the energy centres of our body.*

GREEN Growth, harmony and stability. This generous colour is the colour of innocence and joy, where something new is beginning to form.

PURPLE This aristocratic colour represents transformation of the past, and the faith and knowledge in our own inner centre.

Each culture has an understanding of the meanings for different colours. In the West, our instincts tell us for example, that red is vibrant, symbolizing passion and also danger, whilst green is healthy and symbolizes growth. Different cultures often attach similar meanings to colours, after all, the sky is blue, the grass is green and the night is black no matter where you are in the world.

CHAKRAS

Buddhists and Hindus believe that the body has seven interrelated energy centres, called chakras, that govern the health of our spiritual, mental and physical being. Each chakra is associated with a different colour, physical function and emotional and mental state.

BASE CHAKRA This centre is at the end of the spine, and is linked with the colour red. It represents passion, practicality and the primal energies for survival.

NAVEL CHAKRA This centre, located in the lower abdomen, governs self-worth, self-belief creativity, feelings, pleasure and exploration. Its colour is orange.

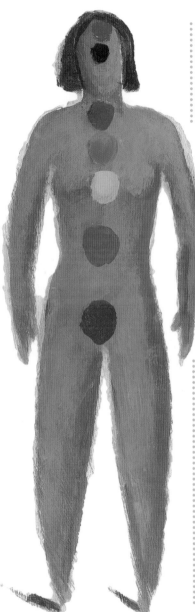

SOLAR PLEXUS CHAKRA This symbolizes self-identity, self-awareness, personal power and independence of being. The colour is yellow.

HEART CHAKRA This is associated with relationships, personal development, responsibility and the ability to give and receive love unconditionally. Its colour is green.

THROAT CHAKRA Light blue in colour this centre represents communication, honest self-expression, the flow of information and offering your talents to the world.

THIRD EYE CHAKRA This is positioned between the eyes. It is where our intuition, perception, mental organisation, imagination and spiritual awareness sits, and is represented by a deep blue colour.

CROWN CHAKRA Positioned at the top of the head, this spot maintains overall balance of the chakra system. It represents wholeness – our connection with the universe and the centre of our whole being. Its colour is purple.

SHAPES AND NUMBERS

The shapes that we see around us, or that we inscribe in a mandala, and numbers that we use every day all have meaning and relevance if we choose to see it.

SHAPES

The way we move a pencil randomly across a piece of paper can show how we feel in that moment. If the movements are harsh and angular then perhaps we have strong emotions, suppressed and bubbling to the surface. If the patterns are soft, spiral or circular then maybe we are feeling more subjective and our emotions are more subtle.

When you look down at the paper always trust your intuition about the shapes that you see. Always believe what your inner voice is saying and not what another person tells you. Basic shapes also have traditional meanings.

CIRCLE: Circles symbolize wholeness and eternity. The inner circle of the mandala represents the deepest, most profound part of ourselves. Its ring forms a barrier, protecting the interior from the outside world.

LINE: A single line can be short, straight and hard or long, curled and soft, determined, or sinuous. Lines are direct expressions of our feelings and emotions. Hard lines often represent repression and pain, softer lines may indicate indecision and lack of motion.

CROSS: The two intersecting lines of a cross symbolize the crossing of two forces within you. They may be equally balanced if the cross is symmetrical or they may be antagonistic where one is dominating the other.

CRESCENT: This is associated with the waxing and waning moon. Waxing represents growing in strength; waning symbolizes loss of power. It speaks of our unconscious and instinctive powers.

TRIANGLE: The three points and sides of a triangle represent your mind, body and spirit. Together, they interact and may move you on to something new, in whichever direction they are pointing.

SQUARE: The four corners and sides of a square represent stability and security. It denotes your inner palace, the solid foundation of your personality that is difficult to shake.

STAR: There are many ways of drawing stars – some are made of triangles, others of crossing lines. They are brilliant signs of hope. Stars remind us of the light that exists within us when times are dark and encourage us not to give up.

SPIRAL: This is an ancient symbol that reminds us of the womb and the protective mothering nature in all of us. It takes us from the broad sweeps of the outer life to an infinitely small centre where we cease to exist.

NUMBERS

Like shapes, numbers, too, have their own symbolism. They can play a role when our inner voice is trying to tell us something and remind us of the way to our centre.

ONE: This is the number of the universe and eternity. It represents the uniqueness of every individual and every moment that we breathe.

TWO: This is the number of opposition and balance and represents equals and decisions. Night and day, sun and moon, each exists in harmony with the other but we must understand where we are in the cycle. Like the balance of the scales, two is the link between opposites where we must decide which path to take.

THREE: Three is the number that represents the eternal balance between life, death and rebirth. It is also representative of our whole selves, the physical, mental and spiritual people that we are.

FOUR: This is the number of change and seasons and the four compass directions. We must always be moving through life, letting the rhythm of its cycles flow through us and carry us on.

FIVE: This is the centre of the wheel and the fifth point in the circle of the four directions. We have five fingers on each hand and five physical senses to interact with the world, and when we stand grounded with our legs apart our body resembles a five-pointed star. Five is the number of connection with the earth, the sky and the present moment.

SIX: This is the number of the four directions, north, south, east and west, plus the two opposites, earth and sky. Infinite creative possibilities are encompassed within these directions. Six is often connected with feminine energies and intuition, the "sixth sense".

SEVEN: There are seven colours of the rainbow, seven notes in the musical scale and seven chakras in the body. Seven is the number of the heavens and the sky and the days of the week. In a mandala it is the number of universal harmony.

EIGHT: This is the number of perfect balance. Eight can be balanced in many ways as an even number. The eight-spoked Dharma Wheel of consciousness in a traditional

Buddhist mandala leads to a perfectly balanced state of awareness.

NINE: This is a number of deep wisdom and knowledge. It is the merging of the three aspects of our being, spiritual, mental and physical, in the most powerful of ways. This is a mystical number, which may be calling you to bring all aspects of your being together.

TEN: This is the number of completion that takes us back to the beginning again. It is a sign of learning that allows us to be reborn into something new and different. It is often regarded as a number of perfection and balance.

TRADITIONAL MANDALA MEDITATION

A mandala is a picture of wholeness and harmony. It has been created from a place of wisdom and contains that essence at its centre. Consequently it is a powerful meditation tool which can help to restore our sense of inner strength and peace. We may use any mandala for meditation – anything from a traditional Buddhist one, to a unique one created entirely by ourselves.

Place the mandala before you, preferably have it hanging in front of you rather than laying on the ground. Make sure it is well lit with natural or natural-coloured light.

Kneel with your back straight, head up, and hands resting comfortably in your lap. Close your mouth and breathe through your nose. Close your eyes. Count ten slow breaths and let your mind become still.

Now open your eyes and focus on the edge of the circle noticing the shapes and colours and what they mean to you. Move your eyes closer to the centre and look at all the intricate patterns of the mandala. Once you have seen something, let it go from your mind and move on to the next pattern.

Continue moving in, seeing and understanding all there is to see, until you reach the centre. Now focus on that smallest point at the centre, and let your mind become still.

Close your eyes and follow the entire journey again in your mind's eye, starting at the outer wall and moving to the centre. See what you remember, what was important to you, and let the rest be forgotten. Don't struggle trying to remember every single detail. Paint the mandala as you recall it in your mind's eye and see its patterns and shapes inside of you.

When you feel ready, mentally place your inner mandala in a special place. This could be somewhere inside of you such as in your heart or belly, or in an imaginary place such as a golden casket, or in a favourite spot you know in nature.

You can go back and reach that mandala anytime that you want to meditate on it again or to be reminded of its beauty and peace.

▼ *You won't be able to meditate successfully unless you are totally relaxed and calm.*

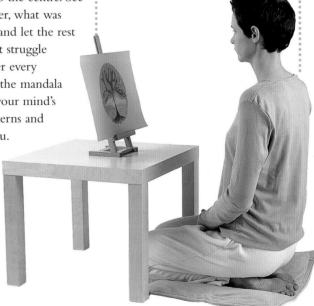

PERSONAL MANDALA MEDITATION

Choose your mandala carefully. A personal mandala does not have to be one that you have created yourself; it can also be a gift from a friend or loved one, or even a print or painting of a traditional mandala that you feel has special significance. Each mandala has its own unique qualities and will impart a very different message. Before you prepare yourself and the room for meditation consider any issues that have been troubling you and select a mandala that you feel will help you to resolve those problems.

Make the room into a meditation room by lighting candles, incense, playing soft and relaxing music and making sure that you have somewhere comfortable to sit. To see into all the depth and subtlety of a personal mandala you must become quiet and still within yourself.

Open your eyes and gaze at the mandala. Let parts of it attract you. Notice shapes, patterns and colours. See what is at the edge and what is at the centre. You may find that defocusing your eyes

▲ *Lighting candles invites beauty into the room. Soft candlelight helps us to defocus when meditating on visual objects.*

slightly will help you see more deeply into the mandala and allow it to "speak to you". Sit and gaze, letting thoughts triggered by the mandala rise and fall, all the time remaining focused on the painting. Spend at least five minutes on this meditation.

Once you feel you have seen everything, close your eyes and remember for a moment the parts

▶ *Our sense of smell has a quick and direct effect on our minds. The smell of incense can help us to relax.*

of the mandala that held the strongest attraction for you. What did those parts mean to you? Did they have any particular messages for you about your life? If so, what can you do now to affect changes in your life in the light of that new knowledge?

When you open your eyes, have in mind one action that you will do in response to listening to your inner voice.

HEALING WITH MANDALAS

Falling ill is an opportunity for us to regrow, just as a tree sheds and regrows its leaves.

Mandalas interact with the centre of our being and from this pivotal point we can effect great changes in our life that will make us healthy, happy and in harmony with the world.

If we change the way we think, we change the way we behave. By changing our behaviour we change our habits. In changing our habits we change the pattern of our whole lives. If we follow the Navajo and Native American belief that all illness begins in the mind, then by changing the way we think

we can also remain healthy and free from sickness.

If we do fall sick, we can at least work towards improving our mental attitude. Whether we are suffering from a mental, physical or spiritual illness, mandalas can help us focus on accepting, listening and then letting go of the pain or sickness.

ACCEPTANCE

Find some quiet time to focus on your self. First lie down, with your hands by your sides and breathe

slowly. Focus on the pain or sickness inside of you. Let it rise to the surface of your mind and body. Now sit and draw a personal mandala of that pain, using the meditation exercise suggested (see Personal Mandala Meditation). Let every emotion and feeling that you have associated with the illness be expressed in the circle. Be true to your pain. If you feel despair try and give the feeling shape and colour on your drawing; if you have flu, imagine what this "looks" like and express it wholeheartedly.

LISTENING

Sit quietly and focus on your mandala. Consider carefully each symbol that you see and what it means to you. Think about your habits and what thoughts and actions may have helped the development of the illness. What can you do differently from now on? Pick a single change that you can make in your life which will lessen the chances of the sickness or pain reoccurring. For example, you may be able to think of a new way of behaving in your job that could reduce your stress levels and susceptibility to flu.

RELEASING

Draw a traditional mandala to contact a place of peace and hope that exists inside of you. Imagine a symbol that represents the change you have decided to try. This could be a tree, an egg or a rainbow, for example, but whatever symbol you choose it is important that it has meaning and feels right for you. Carefully paint or draw that symbol into a mandala with all the positive intention you can muster. By painting the symbol for change on the mandala you are physically working towards making that change in your life. Now meditate on the mandala and hold it in your mind's eye. Whenever you have an opportunity to make the change you have decided upon, remember the mandala and all the positive associations that it holds for you.

By making changes inside of yourself, you affect your life as well as the lives of the people around you. By healing ourselves we bring a little more health and happiness into the world, and the balance of the planet moves closer to a place of harmony too.

▼ *By shedding the old and creating something new inside us we grow closer to our centre.*

CENTRE OF THE MANDALA

At the heart of the mandala is its deepest and most profound point. It is possible to pass this on to others as a gift or to help bring you closer to your own centre of being.

PERSONAL MANDALAS

A personalized mandala is a very special gift honouring another person's qualities. Spend some time thinking about the person

you want to give the mandala to. Meditate as you would for drawing your own personal mandala but think about the recipient rather than yourself. What are their joys and sorrows? Is there a special occasion that you want to honour? What is it about this person that you like? In the circle in your mind, think about the colours which most represent that person and what symbols you associate with your feelings. When you come to create the mandala consider the materials you could use and be creative in your expression of their inner essence.

UNDERSTANDING THE UNIVERSE

You can also create a personal mandala to help bring more understanding into difficult areas of your life. Is there someone with whom you find it hard to interact? Is there a creature that you fear? What things in life or in the world

◀ *By creating mandalas in response to the world around us we can better understand it.*

▲ *Mandalas exist everywhere in the universe; at every scale and in every imaginable medium.*

would you like to understand better? Everything in the universe can be seen as a mandala, we can therefore create a symbolic representation of anything that we like. Through making a personal mandala from the universe, we can reach an understanding of any part of this cosmos in which we live. Focus carefully during your meditation on the person, creature or part of the world that you want to understand. In the circle of your mind's eye, pull in patterns and colours that spontaneously come to

▶ *Just by effecting change in your life, as a ripple spreads outwards, you also effect change in everything you connect with.*

mind. As you paint them, keep your attention focused on that person, creature or situation. Once you have finished, meditate on that inner circle and see what it tells you. You may see the world from the perspective of the other person or you may recognize some of your feelings about them. Listen to what the mandala says to you and the symbols will help guide you to a new place of understanding.

CHANGING YOUR LIFE
By focusing our thoughts on changing an aspect of a mandala so we focus our thoughts on changing our lives. It is through our intent of purpose that we change the way that we live in the world around us. What do you

dream of achieving? What changes do you need to make in your life to take you closer to your dream? Consider one change that you would like to make. Draw a personal mandala focused on that part of your life, the way it is now. Express what it gives you as well as what it denies you. Now put it to one side and draw a second personal mandala. This time focus on your life after this change has occurred. Are you behaving differently? What does this change give you and what does it deny you? By painting this change and by holding the pattern of that second mandala in your mind, you are actively seeking to make it a reality in your life and paving the way for it to happen.

TEACHINGS OF THE MANDALA

The mandala teaches us that in everyone there is a place of beauty. To live in this place is to be happy, healthy and free. This is the life of our dreams. Each one of us has a different dream and it is up to us to realize what is unfulfilled at the centre of us and begin to make the changes in our lives so that we can be content and live at the centre of our dream.

FINDING TRUTH

Mandalas are one of many tools that you can use to guide you to your centre and what burns at the heart of you. No matter which method you use, all require the deepest level of self-honesty. Speak your truth. Speak it loudly to yourself and louder still to everyone around you. It does not matter if no one else believes you. If you know in your heart that you are following your dream then hold on to that belief and you will reach your goal. We can have anything we want, as long as we are true to our centre and our inner self. Paint a mandala of your dreams, of everything that you

want in life. What is the one thing you want to achieve before you die? Paint it and hold it in your mind's eye as a talisman against

▲ *The Dharma Wheel reminds us of the eight states of unconciousness which will allow us to live in true happiness.*

your own doubts. As you reorient your life towards your centre, paint new mandalas which will reveal more and more about your dreams and perhaps show other new possibilities opening up. Take small steps and slowly but surely you will find that you have crossed the mountain and come to rest in the life you always longed for.

LIVING IN TRUTH

On the road to your dream you will find obstacles. Buddhists use the eight-spoked Dharma Wheel to remind us of the right path to our destiny.

▲ *Our lives are a maze, and only by walking our path of truth will we be set free.*

RIGHT BELIEF

This is the belief in ourselves. We must be sure that we are listening to the voice of our inner selves and not that of the ego.

RIGHT RESOLUTION

This is the intent with which we take the steps on the road to our dream. This should always be done with humility.

RIGHT SPEECH

These are the words that we speak on our journey. If we deny our truth and dishonour ourselves, then we will not reach the centre.

RIGHT ACTION

These are the deeds that we do in the pursuit of our dream. If we do not take the necessary action, we can never reach our goal.

RIGHT EFFORT

This is the energy that we use in our lives. If the source of our inner energy is blocked our actions will be half-hearted.

RIGHT PEACE

This is the dream that we hold and the place where we can choose to be.

▲ *Listen to your inner voice; respect the opinions of others, but don't let them persuade you to give up your dream.*

RIGHT THINKING

These are the thoughts that fuel our intent. If we think selfishly or with petty emotions, and are not humble then our intentions can never take us to our centre.

RIGHT LIVING

This reminds us that all our habits, good or bad, can take us closer to or further away from our centre. Right eating, sleeping, exercise and attitudes can all take us closer to our dream.

Afterword

THE MANDALA TRADITIONS of the Buddhists provide us with a wealth of imagery and symbolism – beautiful circles containing palaces and diamonds, guardian spirits, and lotus leaves. However, the essence of the mandala is translated into every language and culture in sand paintings, medicine wheels, rose windows, stone circles and equations of lines that form computer art. Regardless of time or place, every human being holds at their centre the key to unlock their own unique path to happiness.

Mandalas exist all around us, whether it's in the splendour of the dawning sun or the twisting turns of a winding river. Each image gives another glimpse of the peace that can be found when we are living at the centre of ourselves. Each one is an opportunity to learn how to move to that centre and how to live in harmony with the world. We can all be happy and live the life of our dreams if we choose. There is a universal web of life with which we can fall into harmony and live in peace.

A personal mandala is a symbol of our own unique dream. It can take us from the hustle and bustle of the mundane world with its worries and anxieties to a place where we take responsibility for our thoughts, words and deeds. It can enable us to walk in dignity to the centre of our life, where we long to be. The journey is not easy. In any mandala there are circles of fire to be crossed and tombs of old hurts to be unearthed and laid to rest. At the heart of each mandala, however, lies the centre, drawing us on and waiting for us to reach it. As the Buddhists say,

SEE ALL BEINGS AS BUDDHAS;
HEAR ALL SOUNDS AS MANTRAS;
KNOW ALL REALITY AS MANDALA.

SPEAK YOUR TRUTH AND LIVE THE LIFE
OF YOUR DREAMS.

TEMPLATES

Use these templates as guides for making your own mandalas.
Enlarge them on a photocopier, or trace the design and draw a grid of evenly spaced squares
over your tracing. Draw a larger grid onto another piece of paper and copy the outline square by square.
Draw over the lines to make sure they are continuous.

INDEX AND ACKNOWLEDGEMENTS

apples, 25
atoms, 27

Blessingway, 36-9
Buddha, 20, 21, 34
Buddhism, 19, 28, 30-5, 59, 60

Celts, 11, 12, 41
centre of the mandala, 56-7
chakras, 48
China, 8
Christianity, 12, 13
churches, 13
circles, 8, 50
clouds, 24
colours, 34, 48-9
computer art, 23

Dharma Wheel, 58, 59
drawing a mandala, 32-41
dream catchers, 15

Earth, 25
earth mandalas, 45
Egypt, 10
enlightenment, 19

Greek myths, 11

healing, 54-5
Hildegard of Bingen, 13
Hindu yantra, 18
human mandala, 26

illness, 16, 54-5

Jung, Carl, 22

labyrinths, 11
life, changing, 57
living mandalas, 42

mazes, 11, 13
Medicine Wheel, 14-15, 41, 45

meditation, 52-3
Minotaur, 11
modern mandalas, 22-3
molecules, 27

Nasca Lines, 11
Native Americans, 14-17, 36-9, 54
Navajo, 16-17, 36, 39, 54
Newgrange, 10
numbers, 51

Order of the Golden Dawn, 22

personal mandalas, 40-1, 56
pyramids, 10

rainbows, 49
rose window mandalas, 43

sand paintings, 16-17, 20-1, 36, 39, 44
shapes, 50-1
shields, 15
sky, 24
snowflakes, 24
stars, 24
stone circles, 10
Stonehenge, 10
stones, 25

Tao, 8
Tattva Cards, 22
teachings of the mandala, 58-9
Tibet, 19, 20-1, 30, 32
trees, 25
truth, 58-9

universe, 8, 10, 27, 56-7

Wheel of Time, 20-1

yantra, 18
yin-yang symbol, 8

Picture Acknowledgements:
The publishers gratefully acknowledge the following libraries for use of their pictures:

AKG London pp11b & 13bl & r Erich Lessing; pp16t, 22b.
Andy Weber/Tibet Images pp3, 9, 23t, 29.
Axiom pp15t, 16b Guy Marks; p20 B Luther/Tibet Images; pp21b, 61 Ian Cumming/Tibet Images; p21t Vanessa Smith/Tibet Images.
The Bridgeman Art Library p7 Oriental Museum, Durham University, UK; p12l The Board of Trinity College, Dublin, Ireland; p12t The Design Library, New York, USA; p13t Notre Dame, Paris, France/Peter Willi; p19t Oriental Museum, Durham University, UK, p19b Musée Guimet, Paris, France/Giraudon; p26t Leonardo da Vinci/Galleria dell' Accademia, Venice, Italy; p51r Christie's Images, London, UK
ET Archive p17
Fortean p14 Klaus Aarsleff; p50r Janet & Colin Board; p57t
Paul Heussenstamm pp18, 22t
Images p12r
Oxford Scientific Films pp23b & 45bl Steve Littlewood; p25m Ian West; p46 Chris R Sharpe
Science Photo Library p24bl Herman Eisenbeiss; p24t Mehan Kulyk; p26bl Dr A Lesk; p26br Gary Watson; p27tl Ken Eward; p27b, p51l
Skyscan p10l, p11r, p59l
The Stock Market Photo Agency Inc. pp6b, 47, 50c, 59t
Werner Forman Archive pp8, 15l, 58

l=left, r=right, t=top, b=bottom, m=middle